Do You Really Know The Beatles?

A Quiz Book

Brooke Halpin

Copyright © 2010 Brooke Halpin
All rights reserved.

ISBN: 1-4538-4571-2
ISBN-13: 9781453845714

Many thanks to John, Paul, George, and Ringo for the inspiration; Charles Halpin for his encouragement; Robert Fitzpatrick for his friendship; Mark Bloom for his editorial guidance; and the millions of Beatle fans who keep The Beatles' music alive.

Contents

Section 1:	Questions	1
Chapter 1:	The Beginning & Beatlemania	3
Chapter 2:	The Performances/Tours	9
Chapter 3:	The Movies	13
Chapter 4:	The Singles—The Songs—The Albums	17
Chapter 5:	The Paul McCartney Death Hoax	25
Chapter 6:	Finish The Lyrics	29
Chapter 7:	The Solo Years	33
Chapter 8:	And In The End	39
Chapter 9:	Yesterday and Today	43
Section 2:	Questions & Answers	49
Chapter 10:	The Beginning & Beatlemania	51
Chapter 11:	The Performances/Tours	59
Chapter 12:	The Movies	65
Chapter 13:	The Singles—The Songs—The Albums	75
Chapter 14:	The Paul McCartney Death Hoax	87
Chapter 15:	Finish The Lyrics	93
Chapter 16:	The Solo Years	97
Chapter 17:	And In The End	107
Chapter 18:	Yesterday and Today	115
Conclusion:	The final question and answer	129

Introduction

There was nothing like it before, and there will never be anything like it again. The magical chemistry of John, Paul, George, and Ringo. Their music, concerts, and movies. The fans. The way they evolved, grew as musicians, and reinvented themselves. The Beatles. Then, now, and forever.

As The Beatles popularity sustains through time, they attract new fans with each new generation. This book is for Beatle fans of all ages.

You love The Beatles. Some of you experienced The Beatles when they first arrived in America and Beatlemania took the country by storm. Those of you who missed it, know about it, have heard about it, read about it, or may have seen archival footage of The Beatles performing.

You take pride in knowing about The Beatles. But how much do you really know about them? Are you a Beatle expert? Take the challenge and find out how much you know, or don't know about The Beatles.

To accommodate Beatles fans on all levels of knowledge, this book has a mixture of different levels of questions from beginner to intermediate and advanced. To add to the fun, take the quiz with a friend or two!

I hope you enjoy this book and maybe learn a thing or two about The Beatles!

Brooke Halpin
Summer, 2010

Section 1
????Questions????

"What did you see when you were there?"

Chapter 1
The Beginning & Beatlemania

A long time ago in England, natural occurrences were bringing a certain group of teenagers together. No one knew what the outcome would be. Like most teens, they had dreams and aspirations. Unlike most teens, what they experienced went far beyond their wildest imagination. They worked hard, were filled with passion, and never gave up. It took years and a certain individual before Beatlemania would rattle the world. The chemistry was right. It was just a matter of time. And then wham! The Beatles arrived in the Unites States, and easily conquered America.

They were exciting, and different. What? Suits with no collars? Strange haircuts. And the guy playing bass—looks like he's playing some kind of a violin. The way they spoke, and their *music*. It was *all* different, and it swept teens away, far away, into a Beatles filled frenzy called Beatlemania. The Beatles were new, and we claimed them as ours. Our world had changed, forever.

We were hooked. There was no turning back. We wanted The Beatles constantly, and radio stations fed us daily. We bought all of their records, put their pictures on our bedroom walls, and waited to hear interviews filled with their Liverpudlian voices.

Beatlemania. It had begun, and it would never end.

Q1. What was the name of John's first band?
Q2. What city in England are The Beatles from?
Q3. Who is the youngest Beatle?
Q4. What instrument did John play before he played guitar?
Q5. When is Paul's birthday?
Q6. Who was The Beatles drummer before Ringo?
Q7. On what show did The Beatles make their first US TV appearance?
Q8. When is John's birthday?
Q9. Who was The Beatles manager?
Q10. When is George's birthday?
Q11. On what date did The Beatles arrive in the US for the first time?
Q12. When is Ringo's birthday?
Q13. Name the first song The Beatles played on The Ed Sullivan Show.
Q14. On their first US trip, which three cities did The Beatles visit?
Q15. What is Ringo's real name?
Q16. What did The Beatles do on January 1, 1962?
Q17. What is John's middle name?
Q18. In February 1964, why did The Beatles love Miami?
Q19. Who is the New York disc jockey who called himself the 5th Beatle?

Do You Really Know The Beatles?

Q20. Name the band Ringo played with before joining The Beatles.

Q21. Which Beatle traveled to the US before Beatlemania?

Q22. What was the first US radio station to play a Beatles record?

Q23. On what airline did The Beatles travel when they came to the US for the first time?

Q24. What famous American record producer was on the same flight when The Beatles came to the US for the first time?

Q25. Which TV network broadcast The Beatles performance on The Ed Sullivan Show?

Q26. The Beatles were a backup band for what singer in Germany?

Q27. What brand name guitar did John play on The Ed Sullivan Show?

Q28. What was the first Beatles song played on a US radio station?

Q29. What brand name guitar did George play on The Ed Sullivan Show?

Q30. Where did Brian Epstein discover The Beatles?

Q31. What brand name guitar did Paul play on The Ed Sullivan Show?

Q32. What is George's mother's name?

Q33. Name the songs on the first Beatles single released on Capitol Records.

Q34. What brand name drums did Ringo play on The Ed Sullivan Show?

Q35. Who was The Beatles road manager?

Q36. What is Ringo's father's name?
Q37. Before The Beatles wore collarless suit jackets, what did they wear?
Q38. What is John's mother's name?
Q39. Who was The Beatles bass player before Paul?
Q40. What is Paul's mother's name?
Q41. What instrument did Paul play before he played bass?
Q42. Where did Paul meet John?
Q43. Who did George visit when he came to the US before Beatlemania?
Q44. In addition to Decca, what two other international record labels turned down The Beatles?
Q45. When did Paul and John meet?
Q46. What is Paul's father's name?
Q47. How did George meet John?
Q48. Who is the shortest Beatle?
Q49. What is John's father's name?
Q50. Where did George audition for John?
Q51. What does Mike McGear have to do with Paul?
Q52. What is Ringo's mother's name?
Q53. Where did John live when he was a teenager?
Q54. Performing as a duo, what did John and Paul call themselves?
Q55. What is George's father's name?
Q56. What is Paul's middle name?
Q57. What was the name of the band before they changed their name to The Beatles?

Do You Really Know The Beatles?

Q58. In 1964, what did The Beatles launch upon the United States?

Q59. What is Ringo's middle name?

Q60. What is the only song credited to McCartney and Harrison?

Q61. Who did John go to Spain with on holiday in 1963?

Q62. What type of English accent did The Beatles have?

Q63. When they first met, George didn't like something about George Martin. What was it?

Chapter 2
The Performances/Tours

One major element that fueled Beatlemania and record sales was their live performances. The Beatles performed throughout the world and of course, the USA. For those of you who were fortunate enough to experience it, you know The Beatles live performances were unlike any other. The level of hysteria was out of control. With all the screaming, The Beatles could barely hear themselves play! For several reasons, the tours stopped, but the history of The Beatles tours lives on forever.

Q1. Where did The Beatles perform their first live concert in the US?
Q2. Name the American promoter responsible for The Beatles Carnegie Hall performance.
Q3. When did The Beatles perform their first live concert in the US?
Q4. Before coming to the US, where did The Beatles perform for 18 days?
Q5. What brand name amplifiers did The Beatles use on their tours?

Q6. On their 1965 US tour, what was the only song George sang lead vocal?

Q7. When did The Beatles perform at Carnegie Hall?

Q8. How did The Beatles travel from New York City to their 1965 Shea Stadium concert?

Q9. What were The Beatles stage positions?

Q10. Was The Beatles Carnegie Hall performance recorded?

Q11. In 1965, where did The Beatles perform in Los Angeles?

Q12. What was so unusual about the way John played electric piano on "I'm Down," on their 1965 US tour?

Q13. Why wasn't The Beatles 1966 Memphis concert sold out?

Q14. Where was the last US Beatles concert?

Q15. Who was the promoter for The Beatles 1965 Shea Stadium concert?

Q16. In 1966, where did The Beatles perform in Boston?

Q17. How many cities did The Beatles perform in during their 1965 US tour?

Q18. Name the photographer who took pictures of The Beatles last concert performance.

Q19. In 1966, where did The Beatles perform in Tokyo, Japan?

Q20. When was the last US Beatles concert?

Q21. How did The Beatles escape from the fans at their last concert?

Do You Really Know The Beatles?

Q22. How many people attended The Beatles 1965 Shea Stadium concert?

Q23. On their 1966 US tour, what was the only song George sang lead vocal?

Q24. Why did The Beatles get "roughed up" in the Philippines?

Q25. What did George say after their last concert?

Q26. In 1965, where did The Beatles perform in San Francisco?

Q27. How many cities did The Beatles perform in during their 1966 US tour?

Q28. During their 1965 tour, what did The Beatles wear on their jackets?

Q29. What was the main reason why The Beatles stopped touring?

Q30. Where did The Beatles last live performance take place?

Chapter 3
The Movies

Because the demand for The Beatles was so strong, it didn't take long before they appeared on the big screen in feature length films. The Beatles films are filled with some of their great songs, and we got a closer glimpse of their personalities. The movies are funny, witty, playful, and one reveals The Beatles inner tensions. This chapter asks you questions about their movies.

Ready for some action?

Q1. What's the name of The Beatles first movie?
Q2. How many Beatles movies are there?
Q3. In *A Hard Day's Night,* which Beatle is late for a TV rehearsal?
Q4. Name all of The Beatles movies.
Q5. Who directed the movie *Help!*?
Q6. During the opening scene in *A Hard Day's Night*, when The Beatles are running away from fans, which Beatle trips and falls down?
Q7. In *Help!,* what is everyone trying to get from Ringo?
Q8. Who's the "clean old man" in *A Hard Day's Night*?
Q9. The movie *Help!* was shot at three different geographical locations. Name them.
Q10. Who directed *A Hard Day's Night*?

Q11. Name the one and only George Harrison song in the movie *Help!*.

Q12. What are the bad characters in the movie *Yellow Submarine* called?

Q13. Name the actress George met while filming *A Hard Day's Night* who became his significant other.

Q14. In the scene from *Help!*, when Ringo is trapped in a cellar with a tiger, what does everyone sing to calm the tiger down?

Q15. Who composed the orchestral music in the movie *Yellow Submarine*?

Q16. In *A Hard Day's Night*, where did The Beatles perform "I Should Have Know Better"?

Q17. What is the original title to the *Let It Be* movie?

Q18. When was the movie *Magical Mystery Tour* premiered?

Q19. Name the keyboard player who played with The Beatles during the *Let It Be* film.

Q20. What was the original title to the movie *Help!*?

Q21. What is the name of the old man on the bus in *Magical Mystery Tour*?

Q22. At the end of the *Let It Be* movie, where did The Beatles perform?

Q23. Who plays the alto flute solo in "You've Got To Hide Your Love Away" in *Help!*?

Q24. What is the name of the Nowhere Man in *Yellow Submarine*?

Do You Really Know The Beatles?

Q25. In *A Hard Day's Night*, which Beatle gets in trouble with the police?

Q26. In *Help!*, where did The Beatles perform "Another Girl"?

Q27. In the movie *Magical Mystery Tour*, where was "The Fool on The Hill" filmed?

Q28. How many songs does George have on the *Yellow Submarine* soundtrack LP?

Q29. Name the songs written by George on the *Yellow Submarine* soundtrack LP.

Q30. In *Help!*, where did The Beatles perform "The Night Before"?

Q31. Which Beatle invited a keyboard player to join The Beatles during the *Let It Be* film?

Q32. In *Magical Mystery Tour*, what did The Beatles travel in?

Q33. In *Yellow Submarine*, what was John before he was John?

Q34. In 1995, The Beatles released a documentary. What's the name of the documentary?

Q35. Which Beatle came up with the title to their film, *A Hard Day's Night*?

Q36. What is the brand name guitar George played in the movie *A Hard Day's Night*?

Q37. In *Help!*, what color did Ringo have to be before he could be sacrificed?

Q38. Besides The Beatles, what other band performed in *Magical Mystery Tour*?

Q39. In *Let It Be*, what did John say at the end of The Beatles rooftop performance?

Q40. In *A Hard Day's Night*, who is The Beatles manager?

Q41. Who is *Help!* dedicated to?

Chapter 4
The Singles—The Songs—The Albums

It was like magic. The exhilarating sounds of The Beatles coming off the 45 rpm singles and $33^1/_3$ rpm albums and vibrating through a record player's small speaker. You had to have small circular yellow plastic spindles, not to be confused with yellow matter custard, inserted in the center hole in the singles or, better yet, a tall, solid spindle that could accommodate several singles! And the photos of The Beatles on the album covers captured their new look and kept us hooked.

Before the record shops sold the singles and albums, we were knocked out by hearing the latest Beatles songs on the radio. The radio was a direct pipeline to The Beatles. Since The Beatles dominated the Top 40 charts, having a battery operated transistor radio was best because you could carry it with you and hear them! The radio was a major factor in fueling the popularity of The Beatles.

Some of you may still have your original Beatles singles and albums, while others might have 8-track tapes or cassette tapes of their recordings. Most of you probably have The Beatles CD's, and some might have Beatles video tapes and DVD's.

Before you try to answer the questions, if you haven't already done so, I encourage you to listen to the songs. Not only will it help you answer the questions, I know you'll love hearing them again, and again!

Let's find out how much you know about their songs and recordings.

Q1. What are the colors of the label on The Beatles singles released on Capitol Records?

Q2. Which Beatle sings "Do You Want To Know A Secret?"

Q3. Who sings "Honey Don't"?

Q4. What song contains the lyric, "She's happy as can be, you know, she said so."

Q5. On which album is the song, "Devil In Her Heart"?

Q6. Which Beatle sings lead vocal on "Devil In Her Heart"?

Q7. What Lennon/McCartney song was given to Peter Asher and became a number one hit?

Q8. Name the song on the B side of the "Let It Be" single.

Q9. Who is the walrus?

Q10. What was the first Beatle song to use a sitar?

Q11. "Ticket To Ride" is on the A side of the hit single. What song is on the B side?

Q12. Who plays lead guitar on "Get Back"?

Q13. Who produced the *Let It Be* album?

Q14. Name the song that contains the lyric, "The wild and windy night, that the rain washed away."

Q15. Name The Beatles' record producer.

Do You Really Know The Beatles?

Q16. Who wrote the song "Till There Was You"?

Q17. "Till There Was You" is on what album?

Q18. Who wrote "Twist and Shout"?

Q19. Who wrote "Honey Don't"?

Q20. "Honey Don't" is on what Beatles album?

Q21. Name the song that contains the lyric, "The way you treat her, what else can I do."

Q22. What song is on the flipside of the single "Nowhere Man"?

Q23. What record label released The Beatles single "Twist And Shout"?

Q24. On what date was The Beatles' first US single released?

Q25. Where did George write "Blue Jay Way"?

Q26. On what instrument did George write "Blue Jay Way"?

Q27. How did The Beatles come up with the album title, *Rubber Soul*?

Q28. Where was the photo of the *Rubber Soul* album cover taken?

Q29. Which Beatle sings lead vocal on "Act Naturally"?

Q30. What was John's inspiration for writing "Being For The Benefit of Mr. Kite"?

Q31. What Lennon/McCartney song was recorded by The Rolling Stones?

Q32. What is the name of the only Beatle song that uses a fuzz bass?

Q33. Name the song that contains the lyric, "And the eyes in his head see the world spinning around."

Q34. Who plays electric piano on "Get Back"?

Q35. Who is Billy Shears?

Q36. In "I Am The Walrus" what is dripping from a dead dogs eye?

Q37. Who plays the organ on "I'm Looking Through You"?

Q38. Who took the cover photo for the *Meet The Beatles* album?

Q39. What was the name of the record label that released The Beatles first US single?

Q40. What inspired John to write "I Am The Walrus"?

Q41. What song has "Strawberry Fields," "Lady Madonna," and "Fool on the Hill" in the lyrics?

Q42. What two English government officials are mentioned in "Taxman"?

Q43. What was the working title for "Hey Jude"?

Q44. Who sings lead vocal on "What Goes On"?

Q45. Name the songs on The Beatles first US single.

Q46. Why didn't the Beatles single on Vee Jay become a hit?

Q47. What is the name of the only Harrison/Lennon credited song?

Q48. What two things are unusual about the album, *A Hard Day's Night*?

Q49. What is the name of the only album by The Beatles that was recorded in the US?

Q50. Name The Beatles' longest single.

Q51. What song on *The Beatles* (The White Album) does Paul "sing" along with the bass track?

Do You Really Know The Beatles?

Q52. Name the song that contains the lyric, "But what you've got means such a lot to me."

Q53. Who plays the sax solo during the end section on "You Know My Name, Look Up The Number"?

Q54. Who is the eggman?

Q55. When was the album *The Beatles at The Hollywood Bowl* released?

Q56. During the taped recording broadcast of "All You Need is Love," besides singing, what else was John doing?

Q57. What do the songs "Flying," "Dig It," and "Free As A Bird" have in common?

Q58. Name the song that contains the lyric, "How can I ever misplace you?"

Q59. How many weeks was "Hey Jude" number one on the US record charts?

Q60. Name the only Beatles song written by John, Paul, and Ringo.

Q61. How long is The Beatles longest single?

Q62. What is the inspiration for the song "Lucy in the Sky with Diamonds?"

Q63. What songs were on the first Apple label single?

Q64. What do the US *Rubber Soul* and *Sgt. Pepper's Lonely Hearts Club Band* albums have in common?

Q65. What instrument does John play on "Why Don't We Do It in the Road"?

Q66. What was the working title for "I Saw Her Standing There"?

Q67. Where did George write "Here Comes the Sun"?

Q68. What is the inspiration for the song "Penny Lane"?

Q69. What was the working title for "Yesterday"?

Q70. "Good Day Sunshine" was inspired by what Lovin' Spoonful song?

Q71. Who is the inspiration for the song "She Said She Said"?

Q72. Who bangs the anvil on "Maxwell's Silver Hammer"?

Q73. In "I Am The Walrus" who is climbing the Eifel Tower?

Q74. Who plays organ on "I Want You (She's So Heavy)"?

Q75. Who is the inspiration for the song "Hey Jude"?

Q76. Who plays the lead guitar solo in "Good Morning Good Morning"?

Q77. What is the subtitle to "Norwegian Wood"?

Q78. Who plays drums on "Back in the USSR" and "Dear Prudence"?

Q79. What is the original title of the *Revolver* album?

Q80. What is the inspiration for the song "Martha My Dear"?

Q81. Who is Sexy Sadie?

Q82. What songs did The Beatles record that are sung in German?

Q83. Before Capitol Records released it, what label released "She Loves You" in the US?

Do You Really Know The Beatles?

Q84. Paul plays the lead guitar solo on what song on *Revolver*?

Q85. Who recorded "Fool On The Hill" which became a hit single in 1968?

Q86. Who is the inspiration for the song "Dear Prudence"?

Q87. Who was Paul trying to sing like when The Beatles recorded "Long Tall Sally"?

Q88. What record label released the single "Cry For A Shadow"?

Q89. What are John and George singing in the background verse of "Paperback Writer"?

Q90. Who plays piano on the "Revolution" single?

Q91. What is the only Buddy Holly song recorded by The Beatles?

Q92. What are Paul and George singing in the background during "Girl"?

Q93. George has four of his songs on which Beatles album?

Q94. What is the inspiration for the song "Strawberry Fields Forever"?

Q95. "Mark 1" is the working title of what song?

Q96. What does John say in the chorus at the end of "Baby You're A Rich Man" and who is it about?

Q97. Which member of The Rolling Stones sang background vocals on "Yellow Submarine"?

Q98. What are the words in the chorus at the end of "I Am The Walrus"?

Q99. What is The Beatles' longest song?

Q100. During the 1990's, what did The Beatles release that included demos, out takes, and previously unreleased recordings?

Chapter 5
The Paul McCartney Death Hoax

Autumn, 1969, and the sounds of Abbey Road seemed to be everywhere. Any talk about The Beatles coming to an end was nonsense. They were very much alive. And then the news began to spread, oh dear, from radio station to radio station. It was shocking and hard to believe. Paul was dead. Clues about his death were planted in Beatle albums, on the covers, and in the songs.

Caught up in the frenzy, some Beatle lovers dug into the clues. Records on turntables were manually spun backwards, lyrics were studied, album covers analyzed. What they found was fascinating, scary, and heart-breakingly sad. The clues sounded and looked believable. Maybe Paul was really dead.

Were The Beatles in on this? Did they plant the clues and create the death hoax? Some believe they did, to play with our heads. And they were fond of the backwards recording technique, especially John. Some believe they did it to increase record sales. But The Beatles denied having anything to do with it, saying the hoax was nothing but a bunch of concocted rubbish. And all of the clues? Just a coincidence? You decide. Fortunately, Paul is very much alive!

Q1. When you play the beginning of "Revolution No. 9" backwards, what does it say?

Q2. When did Paul supposedly die?

Q3. When you play the gibberish at the end of "I'm So Tired" backwards, what does it say?

Q4. How did Paul supposedly die?

Q5. At the end of "Strawberry Fields Forever," in support of the death hoax, what does John say?

Q6. When you play the ending chorus to "I Am the Walrus" backwards, what does it say?

Q7. When Paul supposedly died, who replaced him?

Q8. How did The Beatles introduce Paul's replacement?

Q9. When you play the chorus to "Let It Be" backwards, what does it say?

Q10. What track on The White Album has the sound of a car crash?

Q11. In support of the Paul is Dead hoax, what does a voice say at the end of "I Am the Walrus"?

Q12. What is a clue on the *Sgt. Pepper* album cover?

Q13. What is another clue on the *Sgt. Pepper* album cover?

Q14. According to the death hoax, why was the album called *Sgt. Pepper's Lonely Hearts Club Band*?

Q15. What is another clue on the *Sgt. Pepper* album cover?

Q16. What is the clue on the inside photo of *Sgt. Pepper*?

Q17. What is the Paul is Dead clue in "A Day in the Life"?

Q18. What is the Paul is Dead clue in "Don't Pass Me By"?

Q19. What is a Paul is Dead clue on the inside photo of *Magical Mystery Tour* of The Beatles dressed in White tuxedos?

Q20. What do the opening lyrics to "She's Leaving Home" have to do with the death hoax?

Q21. What is another clue on one of the inside photos of *Magical Mystery Tour*?

Q22. What clue does George give us on the back of the *Sgt. Pepper* album?

Q23. What is a Paul is Dead clue on the *Abbey Road* album?

Q24. What is another clue on the *Abbey Road* album?

Q25. What is a Paul is Dead clue on the *Let It Be* album?

Q26. Where did a *Life Magazine* reporter find Paul alive?

Chapter 6
Finish The Lyrics

What makes a great song is the perfect combination of music and lyrics. Obviously, The Beatles were masters in putting the two together.

Some of you have heard the songs too many times to count, but do you really know the lyrics to The Beatles songs? Let's find out!

1. I once had a girl, or should I say…_____
2. And she called herself Lil, but everyone knew her as…_____
3. Silently closing her bedroom door, leaving a note…_____
4. Going to work, don't want to go, feeling…_____
5. I've got no time for you right now…_____
6. Carve your number on my wall and maybe you will…_____
7. Waits at the window, wearing the face that she keeps…_____
8. I've got a chip on my shoulder that's…_____
9. Your lips are moving…_____
10. And these memories lose their meaning when I…_____
11. Tried to please her, she only played…_____
12. A crowd of people turned away, but I…_____
13. Your voice is soothing_____

14. Pools of sorrow, waves of joy are... _____
15. A, B, C, D, can I.... _____
16. Nothing you can say, but you can learn... _____
17. Bright are the stars that shine... _____
18. You say you've seen seven wonders and your...
_____
19. She's sweeter than all the girls and... _____
20. If you're feeling sorry and sad, I really... _____
21. What did you see when you were there? Nothing... _____
22. I think of her, but she... _____
23. Leave it till tomorrow to unpack my case, honey... _____
24. Buys every rock and roll book on the... _____
25. Finally made the plane into Paris, honeymooning... _____
26. Ask a policeman on the street. There's... _____
27. The Hendersons will dance and sing as... _____
28. Take these sunken eyes and... _____
29. Say you don't need no diamond rings and... __
30. I never give you my pillow, I only send you... __
31. One and one and one is three, got to be good looking... _____
32. The queen was in the playroom painting pictures for... _____
33. The clouds will be a daisy chain, so... _____
34. And though the holes are rather small... _____
35. You didn't run, you didn't hide, you knew I wanted... _____

Do You Really Know The Beatles?

36. Saving up your money for a rainy day, giving all your…_____
37. She'll never hurt me, she won't desert me…__
38. Don't pay money just to see yourself with…__
39. Lying with his eyes while his hands are busy…__
40. Working for peanuts is all very fine…_____
41. Love you everyday girl…_____
42. I'm taking the time for a number of things that…_____
43. The man with a thousand voices…_____
44. She takes her time and doesn't feel she has to hurry…_____
45. And she promises the earth to me and I believe her…_____
46. All the girls around her say she's got it coming…_____
47. Me used to be angry young man…_____
48. Looking through the bent backed tulips to see…_____
49. She feels good, she knows she's looking fine…
_____
50. Well you may be a lover but…_____
51. If you're listening to this song, you may think…_____
52. The girl that's driving me mad…_____
53. When I hold you in my arms and I feel…_____
54. You think you know me but…_____
55. You'll have to have them all pulled out after…_____

56. It's a thousand pages, give or take a few...___
57. When I get near you..._____
58. I would remember all the things we planned...__
59. Listen to me one more time..._____
60. Try to realize it's all within yourself..._____

Chapter 7
The Solo Years

The solo albums by former Beatles were coveted by most Beatle fans—it was the closest they could get to another Beatles album. But the solo albums also caused division among Beatle fans. John fans wrote Paul off as a silly love song writer and considered John to be the true rock and roller. Paul fans thought John's songs weren't as good as Paul's. George fans believed George was the deepest songwriter. And everyone loved Ringo's solo recordings without comparing him to the other Beatles.

While there are certainly outstanding solo songs by all four former Beatles, it would be hard to argue that what they created together as The Beatles was better. Rumors went on for years that The Beatles were going to get back together and record another album. While listening to their solo recordings, many hoped and wondered, what would the new Beatles album sound like? The answer, more than likely, would have been outstanding. Unfortunately, as history has played out, it never happened, and we'll never know. And what do you know about the solo years?

Q1. What was John's first solo single?
Q2. What color is the Apple label on the *All Things Must Pass* LP?
Q3. What was Paul's first solo single?

Q4. In 1974, John Lennon made a guest appearance at Madison Square Garden. Who did he perform with?

Q5. How many records are in George's *All Things Must Pass* LP?

Q6. What's the name of Ringo's first solo single?

Q7. Where did Paul record his *RAM* LP?

Q8. What was John's second solo single?

Q9. Who produced the *All Things Must Pass* LP?

Q10. What Ringo single can be interpreted as an attack on Paul?

Q11. Who plays lead guitar on "Cold Turkey"?

Q12. Name the song on the flipside of Paul's "Another Day" single.

Q13. Where was John's first concert performance without The Beatles?

Q14. There's one song written by George and Bob Dylan on the *All Things Must Pass* LP. Name the song.

Q15. What's the name of the band Paul formed in 1971?

Q16. What is the name of the band John formed while The Beatles were still officially together?

Q17. What solo song did John release in February, 1970?

Q18. Who is the grand old painter Paul sings about on the *Band on the Run* LP?

Q19. What is the color of the Apple label on John's *Plastic Ono Band* LP?

Q20. What was George's second US single release?

Do You Really Know The Beatles?

Q21. Why is there an explosive sound at the end of "Remember"?

Q22. What is the name of George's second solo LP?

Q23. Who plays drums on the "Instant Karma" single?

Q24. What three songs did John play at Madison Square Garden in 1974?

Q25. Who plays piano on "God" on the *Plastic Ono Band* LP?

Q26. What is the name of the club John got thrown out of in 1974 in West Los Angeles?

Q27. What's the name of the single from Paul's *RAM* LP?

Q28. What solo John song references Paul's death hoax?

Q29. What's the name of Ringo's second solo single?

Q30. Who are the original band members of Wings?

Q31. Where was "Give Peace A Chance" recorded?

Q32. Who wrote "It Don't Come Easy"?

Q33. What hit single by Paul and Wings is on the *Red Rose Speedway* LP?

Q34. What is the second single released from the *Double Fantasy* album?

Q35. Which solo Beatle album is the closest to a Beatles reunion and has all four Beatles on it?

Q36. Who produced "It Don't Come Easy"?

Q37. What Lennon/McCartney song did Elton John record and release as a single?

Q38. George was slapped with a lawsuit because of what solo song?

Q39. Who played piano on "It Don't Come Easy"?

Q40. On George's *The Concert For Bangladesh* LP and at the concert, there were two drummers. Ringo was one, who was the other?

Q41. What's another word for George's song "Wah-Wah"?

Q42. Where did John celebrate his 31st birthday?

Q43. Who produced "Photograph"?

Q44. In addition to John, who else plays acoustic guitar on "Give Peace A Chance"?

Q45. Who wrote "Photograph"?

Q46. Where was *The Concert for Bangladesh* performed and recorded?

Q47. Paul recorded some of the *Tug of War* album on what island?

Q48. Who was the opening act at *The Concert for Bangladesh*?

Q49. Who was with John at The Troubadour in 1974?

Q50. "Listen to What the Man Said" is on what Wings LP?

Q51. Where did John and Yoko record their *Double Fantasy* LP?

Q52. "Silly Love Songs" is on what Wings LP?

Q53. When and where was John's last live concert performance?

Q54. On what label was *Double Fantasy* released?

Do You Really Know The Beatles?

Q55. Who sings "Ebony and Ivory" with Paul on the *Tug of War* LP?

Q56. What song was the first hit single from John & Yoko's *Double Fantasy* LP?

Q57. What's the name of the song Paul wrote for a James Bond movie?

Q58. Who produced the *Tug of War* LP?

Q59. Who sang the "No No Song"?

Q60. Who co-wrote and sings the hit song "Say, Say, Say" with Paul?

Q61. According to George, what are Apple Scruffs?

Q62. What song did Paul write as a tribute to John?

Q63. Who produced the "No No Song"?"

Q64. Who played rhythm guitars and sang background vocals at *The Concert for Bangladesh*?

Q65. What LP is "Say, Say, Say" on?

Q66. Why was John thrown out of The Troubadour?

Q67. What is the song on the flipside of the single "My Love"?

Q68. What song did George write as a tribute to John?

Q69. Paul's song "No More Lonely Nights" is in what movie?

Q70. Who is Dr. Winston O'Boogie?

Chapter 8
And In The End

Nothing lasts forever, or as George had said, all things must pass. Even The Beatles. The breakup of The Beatles was a tough pill to swallow. Nobody wanted them to split, except for The Beatles themselves. One of the reasons why they lasted as long as they did was because they evolved and progressed as a single entity—as a band. Eventually, the evolving Beatles went off on their own, without the others, and no longer functioned as a group. Four strong individuals blossomed. In the beginning it was always about the band The Beatles, not four individuals.

As they evolved and changed, tensions between them set in. John was completely captivated with Yoko and was recording without Paul, George, and Ringo. George was producing other artists and getting deeper into Indian mysticism and transcendental meditation, Ringo was acting in movies, and Paul was trying to keep The Beatles together. The more Paul tried, the more John, George, and Ringo resisted. And there were major business problems with The Beatles' company Apple. With all the divisive changes taking place, Paul wanted to get back to what it was like when they were a group playing rock and roll. But it was too late. The Beatles couldn't "get back."

Q1. What was the first thing that happened that set The Beatles free from being a group?

Q2. Which album signaled the beginning of the end?

Q3. Who was the first to temporarily quit The Beatles?

Q4. Was Yoko solely responsible for the breakup of The Beatles?

Q5. After the *Magical Mystery Tour* album, as song writers, what had changed between John and Paul?

Q6. Who broke up The Beatles?

Q7. What was the name of The Beatles failing clothing boutique?

Q8. When did The Beatles officially breakup?

Q9. Why did Ringo temporarily quit The Beatles?

Q10. Who was the second to temporarily quit the band?

Q11. What were the signs of The Beatles breaking up on The White Album?

Q12. Who did Paul want to manage Apple and The Beatles?

Q13. What was the last album recorded by The Beatles?

Q14. Why was *Let It Be* released after *Abbey Road*?

Q15. Why did George temporarily quit The Beatles?

Q16. Who produced the final version of the *Let It Be* album?

Q17. Who did John, George, and Ringo want to manage Apple and The Beatles?

Do You Really Know The Beatles?

Q18. What was the original name of the *Let It Be* Album?

Q19. How did Paul know Lee Eastman?

Q20. What band was Jeff Lynne and George Harrison in?

Q21. What were the last two songs The Beatles recorded and released?

Q22. What did Paul think of the way Phil Spector produced "The Long and Winding Road"?

Q23. Who produced "Free As a Bird" and "Real Love"?

Q24. When The Beatles recorded "Free As A Bird" and "Real Love," was John in the studio?

Q25. Where did John and Yoko live in New York City?

Q26. Besides Jeff Lynne and George, who else was in The Traveling Wilburys?

Q27. When did George die?

Q28. What was the name of the memorial concert for George?

Q29. When did John die?

Q30. How did George die?

Q31. How did John die?

Q32. Where was George when he died?

Q33. Who shot John?

Q34. Where was John when he got shot?

Q35. Where is Strawberry Fields in New York City?

Q36. When was the Concert For George?

Q37. At the Concert For George, who sang "For You Blue," "Something," and "All Things Must Pass"?

Q38. Where did the Concert For George take place?

Q39. At the Concert For George, what songs did Ringo sing?

Q40. At the Concert For George, who sang "While My Guitar Gently Weeps"?

Q41. At the Concert For George, who sang "My Sweet Lord"?

Q42. At the Concert For George, who sang "Taxman"?

Q43. How did The Beatles record "Free As a Bird" and "Real Love" without John?

Q44. At the Concert For George, who sang "Wah-Wah"?

Q45. What was the last song at the Concert For George?

Q46. At the Concert For George, who sang "I'll See You In My Dreams"?

Q47. In honor of George, on April 14, 2009, Paul, Olivia and Dhani Harrison were in Hollywood for what special occasion?

Chapter 9
Yesterday And Today

The longevity and appeal of The Beatles span decades. They are timeless; they are classic. Their popularity increases with each new generation of young fans. More than likely, their music will last indefinitely. The Beatles are yesterday, today, and tomorrow.

Can you answer these yesterday and today questions?

Q1. Who was George's first wife?
Q2. Who recorded the Lennon/McCartney song "Bad To Me"?
Q3. Who was Paul engaged to but never married?
Q4. What brand name guitar did Paul play during the "All You Need Is Love" broadcast?
Q5. Who was George's sitar teacher?
Q6. Who was John's first wife?
Q7. How did The Beatles come up with the name Billy Shears?
Q8. Who recorded The Lennon/McCartney song "World Without Love"?
Q9. Who is Ringo's second wife?
Q10. Who is Sean Lennon?
Q11. Which Beatle wore glasses?
Q12. What was the address of The Beatles Apple Corps Ltd. company?

Q13. Name George's second wife.

Q14. Who was the link between The Beatles and Billy J. Kramer and The Dakotas?

Q15. Who introduced George to Indian music?

Q16. Where did John and Yoko get married?

Q17. Who recorded the Lennon/McCartney song "From A Window"?

Q18. Who is Stu Sutcliffe?

Q19. Where did Donovan and The Beatles go together?

Q20. In addition to "World Without Love," what other Lennon/McCartney song did Peter and Gordon record?

Q21. Who was Ringo's first wife?

Q22. Who introduced The Beatles to marijuana?

Q23. Who wrote the song "Woman" for Peter and Gordon?

Q24. What is the name of John and Cynthia's son?

Q25. Which Beatle is left handed?

Q26. Who was the link between The Beatles and Peter and Gordon?

Q27. Name the second solo album released by a Beatle while The Beatles were still together.

Q28. What song did George write with Eric Clapton that was recorded by Cream?

Q29. What Las Vegas theatrical production is based on Beatle songs?

Q30. Who did The Beatles meet in Germany who became a member of John's Plastic Ono Band?

Q31. While still a Beatle, Paul composed soundtrack music to what movie?

Do You Really Know The Beatles?

Q32. Which Beatle has blue eyes?

Q33. Before The Beatles became famous, what European city and country did they perform in?

Q34. When Paul moved to London in 1964, where did he live?

Q35. Who was the first Beatle to release a solo album while The Beatles were still together?

Q36. Who performs the Las Vegas theatrical production based on Beatle songs?

Q37. In 2001, Paul performed at fund raising events for what charitable organization?

Q38. What was Billy J. Kramer and The Dakotas' first big hit that was written by Lennon/ McCartney?

Q39. Who was a working girl, north of England way?

Q40. How did the Cirque du Soleil production of LOVE happen?

Q41. Who died in the church and was buried along with her name?

Q42. Which member of Cream married George's first wife?

Q43. If you're down, who will pick you up?

Q44. Who mixed the LOVE soundtrack and CD?

Q45. Who is Paul's second wife?

Q46. Who has sea shell eyes and a windy smile?

Q47. Name the first solo album released by a Beatle while The Beatles were still together.

Q48. Who is Giles Martin?

Q49. Who played drums with John at The Rolling Stones Rock and Roll Circus?

Q50. What is the song "Cold Turkey" about?

Q51. What does Desmond take to get to the jewelers store?

Q52. Who is Beatrice McCartney?

Q53. Who played bass guitar with John at The Rolling Stones Rock and Roll Circus?

Q54. Who is the all American bullet-headed Saxon mother's son?

Q55. Who wrote and produced the song "Come And Get It"?

Q56. Who doesn't have a point of view, and knows not where he's going to?

Q57. Who played lead guitar with John at The Rolling Stones Rock and Roll Circus?

Q58. Who is singing in the dead of night?

Q59. When the rain comes, what do they do?

Q60. What song did John sing at The Rolling Stones Rock and Roll Circus?

Q61. Are Paul and Heather still married?

Q62. Who is the professional female photographer that took pictures of The Beatles in Germany?

Q63. Jojo left his home in Tucson Arizona for what?

Q64. What college did John and Stu Sutcliffe attend?

Q65. For which Beatle album cover did Klaus Voormann do the art work?

Q66. Who came in, grinning a grin?

Q67. What happened to Stu Sutcliffe?

Q68. Who is filling in a ticket in her little white book?

Do You Really Know The Beatles?

Q69. Who produced and arranged "Those Were The Days"?

Q70. Who is so good looking but she looks like a man?

Q71. Who was Stu Sutcliffe's girlfriend?

Q72. Who is majoring in medicine?

Q73. Who plays drums on "The Ballad of John and Yoko"?

Q74. Who has cellophane flowers of yellow and green, towering over her head?

Q75. What's the name of Ringo's band?

Q76. Who listens to the music playing in her head?

Q77. Where did John meet Cynthia Powell?

Q78. Who are clutching forks and knives to eat their bacon?

Q79. How many children does Ringo have?

Q80. Who was The Beatles first music publisher?

Q81. What was she protected by when she came in through the bathroom window?

Q82. What does Paul do during the song "I'm Only Sleeping"?

Q83. Ringo and Peter Sellers co-starred in what movie?

Q84. What does John say at the beginning of "Let It Be" on the album version?

Q85. Who sings "Those Were The Days"?

Q86. What Apple recording artist recorded "Come and Get It"?

Q87. What street doesn't Maggie Mae walk down anymore?

Q88. How many children does Paul have?

Q89. Who says something at the end of "Helter Skelter" and what does he say?

Q90. Rose and Valerie are doing what in the gallery?

Q91. Before moving to The Dakota, where did John and Yoko live?

Q92. In 1977, what band released an album that was rumored to be The Beatles?

Q93. When the rain comes, besides hiding their head, what else do they do?

Q94. What is the name of George's only child?

Q95. Who wrote the lyrics to "Those Were The Days"?

Q96. What do the Indra Club, the Kaiserkeller, the Top Ten Club, and the Star Club have in common?

Q97. What song was going to be released as a new Beatles single on *Anthology 3*?

Q98. Mary Hopkin had a hit single written by Paul (credited to Lennon/McCartney). Name the song.

Q99. Where and when did John meet Yoko?

Q100. What Beatle song has some verses in French?

Q101. What does Ringo play on the US single "Love Me Do"?

Q102. What did Seltaeb have to do with The Beatles?

Q103. In 2010, who were the musicians playing in Paul's band?

Section 2
Questions & Answers

To make it easy for you, the questions precede the answers, so you don't have to flip through pages to find the corresponding questions.

Chapter 10
The Beginning & Beatlemania

"Where are we going, fellas?"
"To the top, Johnny!"
"Where's that, fellas?"
"To the toppermost of the poppermost!"

Q1. What was the name of John's first band?
A1. The Quarrymen

Q2. What city in England are The Beatles from?
A2. Liverpool

Q3. Who is the youngest Beatle?
A3. George

Q4. What instrument did John play before he played guitar?
A4. Banjo

Q5. When is Paul's birthday?
A5. June 18, 1942

Q6. Who was The Beatles drummer before Ringo?

A6. Pete Best

Q7. On what show did The Beatles make their first US TV appearance?
A7. The Ed Sullivan Show

Q8. When is John's birthday?
A8. October 9, 1940

Q9. Who was The Beatles manager?
A9. Brian Epstein

Q10. When is George's birthday?
A10. February 25, 1943

Q11. On what date did The Beatles arrive in the US for the first time?
A11. February 7, 1964

Q12. When is Ringo's birthday?
A12. July 7, 1940

Q13. Name the first song The Beatles played on The Ed Sullivan Show.
A13. "All My Loving"

Q14. On their first US trip, which three cities did The Beatles visit?
A14. New Your, Washington DC, and Miami

Q15. What is Ringo's real name?

Do You Really Know The Beatles?

A15. Richard Starkey

Q16. What did The Beatles do on January 1, 1962?
A16. They recorded an audition tape at Decca Records in London.

Q17. What is John's middle name?
A17. Winston, named after Winston Churchill.

Q18. In February 1964, why did The Beatles love Miami?
A18. Because it was sunny and warm!

Q19. Who is the New York disc jockey who called himself the 5th Beatle?
A19. Murray the K

Q20. Name the band Ringo played with before joining The Beatles.
A20. Rory Storm and The Hurricanes

Q21. Which Beatle traveled to the US before Beatlemania?
A21. George. In September 1963, he traveled to Benton, Illinois.

Q22. What was the first US radio station to play a Beatles record?
A22. WWDC in Washington, DC, on December 17, 1963. This happened as the result of a listener named Marsha Albert who called disc jockey

Carroll James and asked that he play any Beatles record.

Q23. On what airline did The Beatles travel when they came to the US for the first time?
A23. PAN AM (Pan American)

Q24. What famous American record producer was on the same flight when The Beatles came to the US for the first time?
A24. Phil Spector

Q25. Which TV network broadcast The Beatles performance on The Ed Sullivan Show?
A25. CBS

Q26. The Beatles were a backup band for what singer in Germany?
A26. Tony Sheridan

Q27. What brand name guitar did John play on The Ed Sullivan Show?
A27. A black Rickenbacker

Q28. What was the first Beatles song played on a US radio station?
A28. "I Want To Hold Your Hand"

Q29. What brand name guitar did George play on The Ed Sullivan Show?
A29. A Gretsch Country Gentleman

Do You Really Know The Beatles?

Q30. Where did Brian Epstein discover The Beatles?
A30. The Cavern

Q31. What brand name guitar did Paul play on The Ed Sullivan Show?
A31. A Hofner bass

Q32. What is George's mother's name?
A32. Louise

Q33. Name the songs on the first Beatles single released on Capitol Records.
A33. "I Want To Hold Your Hand" and "I Saw Her Standing There"

Q34. What brand name drums did Ringo play on The Ed Sullivan Show?
A34. A Ludwig drum kit

Q35. Who was The Beatles road manager?
A35. Mal Evans

Q36. What is Ringo's father's name?
A36. Richard

Q37. Before The Beatles wore collarless suit jackets, what did they wear?
A37. Black leather jackets

Q38. What is John's mother's name?

A38. Julia

Q39. Who was The Beatles bass player before Paul?
A39. Stu Sutcliffe

Q40. What is Paul's mother's name?
A40. Mary

Q41. What instrument did Paul before he played bass?
A41. Guitar and piano

Q42. Where did Paul meet John?
A42. At a church festival at St. Peter's in Woolton, a section of Liverpool

Q43. Who did George visit when he came to the US before Beatlemania?
A43. His sister Louise

Q44. In addition to Decca, what two other international record labels turned down The Beatles?
A44. Columbia, and Capitol

Q45. When did Paul and John meet?
A45. July 6, 1957

Q46. What is Paul's father's name?
A46. James

Do You Really Know The Beatles?

Q47. How did George meet John?
A47. Paul introduced George to John

Q48. Who is the shortest Beatle?
A48. Ringo

Q49. What is John's father's name?
A49. Fred

Q50. Where did George audition for John?
A50. On the upper level of a double-decker bus

Q51. What does Mike McGear have to do with Paul?
A51. He is Paul's brother, Peter Michael McCartney

Q52. What is Ringo's mother's name?
A52. Elsie

Q53. Where did John live when he was a teenager?
A53. At his Aunt Mimi's house

Q54. Performing as a duo, what did John and Paul call themselves?
A54. The Nerk Twins

Q55. What is George's father's name?
A55. Harold

Q56. What is Paul's middle name?

A56. Paul. His first name is James.

Q57. What was the name of the band before they changed their name to The Beatles?
A57. The Silver Beatles

Q58. In 1964, what did The Beatles launch upon the United States?
A58. The British Invasion

Q59. What is Ringo's middle name?
A59. Bernard

Q60. What is the only song credited to McCartney and Harrison?
A60 "In Spite of All the Danger"

Q61. Who did John go to Spain with on holiday in 1963?
A61. Brian Epstein

Q62. What type of English accent did The Beatles have?
A62. Scouse

Q63. When they first met, George didn't like something about George Martin. What was it?
A63. His tie

Chapter 11
The Performances/Tours

"We'd like to do a song from our…"

Q1. Where did The Beatles perform their first live concert in the US?
A1. At the Washington, DC Coliseum

Q2. Name the American promoter responsible for The Beatles Carnegie Hall performance.
A2. Sid Bernstein. In November 1963, he spoke with Brian Epstein and presented the idea to him. It was a bold move. At the time, few Americans had ever heard of The Beatles, and prior to The Beatles Carnegie Hall performance, no rock and roll act had ever performed there.

Q3. When did The Beatles perform their first live concert in the US?
A3. February 11, 1964

Q4. Before coming to the US, where did The Beatles perform for 18 days?
A4. The Olympia Theater in Paris

Q5. What brand name amplifiers did The Beatles use on their tours?
A5. Vox

Q6. On their 1965 US tour, what was the only song George sang lead vocal?
A6. "Everybody's Trying To Be My Baby"

Q7. When did The Beatles perform at Carnegie Hall?
A7. February 12, 1964

Q8. How did The Beatles travel from New York City to their 1965 Shea Stadium concert?
A8. In a helicopter. It was the best way to get to the stadium to avoid getting crushed by the fans!

Q9. What were The Beatles stage positions?
A9. John stage left, George center, Ringo center rear, on platform, Paul stage right.

Q10. Was The Beatles Carnegie Hall performance recorded?
A10. No. Even though there was a deal between Capitol Records and Carnegie Hall to have George Martin record it, it never happened. The American Federation of Musicians blocked the recording because George Martin was not a union member.

Do You Really Know The Beatles?

Q11. In 1965, where did The Beatles perform in Los Angeles?
A11. The Hollywood Bowl

Q12. What was so unusual about the way John played electric piano on "I'm Down," on their 1965 US tour?
A12. He played it with his elbow!

Q13. Why wasn't The Beatles 1966 Memphis sold out?
A13. Because some teens boycotted the concert because of John's statement about The Beatles being more popular than Jesus.

Q14. Where was the last US Beatles concert?
A14. Candle Stick Park, San Francisco

Q15. Who was the promoter for The Beatles 1965 Shea Stadium concert?
A15. Sid Bernstein

Q16. In 1966, where did The Beatles perform in Boston?
A16. Suffolk Downs Racetrack

Q17. How many cities did The Beatles perform in during their 1965 US tour?
A17. Nine

Q18. Name the photographer who took pictures of The Beatles last concert performance.
A18. Jim Marshall

Q19. In 1966, where did The Beatles perform in Tokyo, Japan?
A19. At the Budokan Arena

Q20. When was the last US Beatles concert?
A20. August 29, 1966

Q21. How did The Beatles escape from the fans at their last concert?
A21. In a Wells Fargo armored truck.

Q22. How many people attended The Beatles 1965 Shea Stadium concert?
A22. 55,600

Q23. On their 1966 US tour, what was the only song George sang lead vocal?
A23. "If I Needed Someone"

Q24. Why did The Beatles get "roughed up" in the Philippines?
A24. Because they turned down a breakfast invitation at the Presidential Palace and didn't meet with First Lady Imelda Marcos.

Do You Really Know The Beatles?

Q25. What did George say after their last concert?
A25. "I'm no longer a Beatle."

Q26. In 1965, where did The Beatles perform in San Francisco?
A26. The Cow Palace

Q27. How many cities did The Beatles perform in during their 1966 US tour?
A27. Thirteen

Q28. During their 1965 tour, what did The Beatles wear on their jackets?
A28. A Wells Fargo agent badge.

Q29. What was the main reason why The Beatles stopped touring?
A29. It had become too dangerous. Death threats were made against John.

Q30. Where did The Beatles last live performance take place?
A30. On the rooftop of their office building in London.

Chapter 12
The Movies

"You're a swine."

Q1. What's the name of The Beatles first movie?
A1. *A Hard Day's Night*

Q2. How many Beatles movies are there?
A2. Five

Q3. In *A Hard Day's Night*, which Beatle is late for a TV rehearsal?
A3. Ringo

Q4. Name all of The Beatles movies.
A4. *A Hard Day's Night, Help!, Magical Mystery Tour, Yellow Submarine,* and, *Let It Be*

Q5. Who directed the movie *Help!*?
A5. Richard Lester

Q6. During the opening scene in *A Hard Day's Night*, when The Beatles are running away from fans, which Beatle trips and falls down?
A6. George

Q7. In *Help!*, what is everyone trying to get from Ringo?
A7. The sacred ring

Q8. Who's the "clean old man" in *A Hard Day's Night*?
A8. Paul's grandfather

Q9. The movie *Help!* was shot at three different geographical locations. Name them.
A9. England, the Swiss Alps, the Caribbean

Q10. Who directed *A Hard Day's Night?*
A10. Richard Lester

Q11. Name the one and only George Harrison song in the movie *Help!*.
A11. "I Need You"

Q12. What are the bad characters in the movie *Yellow Submarine* called?
A12. Blue Meanies

Q13. Name the actress George met while filming *A Hard Day's Night* who became his significant other.
A13. Pattie Boyd, who became Mrs. George Harrison

Do You Really Know The Beatles?

Q14. In the scene from *Help!* when Ringo is trapped in a cellar with a tiger, what does everyone sing to calm the tiger down?
A14. The "Ode to Joy" chorus from Beethoven's 9th Symphony

Q15. Who composed the orchestral music in the movie *Yellow Submarine*?
A15. George Martin

Q16. In *A Hard Day's Night,* where did The Beatles perform "I Should Have Know Better"?
A16. In a cargo train car

Q17. What is the original title to the *Let It Be* movie?
A17. Get Back

Q18. When was the movie *Magical Mystery Tour* premiered?
A18. December 26, 1967

Q19. Name the keyboard player who played with The Beatles during the *Let It Be* film.
A19. Billy Preston

Q20. What was the original title to the movie *Help!*?
A20. *Eight Arms to Hold You*

Q21. What is the name of the old man on the bus in *Magical Mystery Tour*?
A21. Mr. Bloodvessel

Q22. At the end of the *Let It Be* movie, where did The Beatles perform?
A22. On a rooftop

Q23. Who plays the alto flute solo in "You've Got To Hide Your Love Away" in *Help!*?
A23. The indoor gardener

Q24. What is the name of the Nowhere Man in *Yellow Submarine*?
A24. Jeremy Hilary Boob

Q25. In *A Hard Day's Night*, which Beatle gets in trouble with the police?
A25. Ringo

Q26. In *Help!*, where did The Beatles perform "Another Girl"?
A26. On a bunch of rocks

Q27. In the movie *Magical Mystery Tour*, where was "The Fool on The Hill" filmed?
A27. On a hilltop near Nice, France

Q28. How many songs does George have on the *Yellow Submarine* soundtrack LP?
A28. Two

Do You Really Know The Beatles?

Q29. Name the songs written by George on the *Yellow Submarine* soundtrack LP.
A29. "Only A Northern Song" and "It's All Too Much"

Q30. In *Help!*, where did The Beatles perform "The Night Before"?
A30. On an outdoor platform in an open field

Q31. Which Beatle invited a keyboard player to join The Beatles during the *Let It Be* film?
A31. George

Q32. In *Magical Mystery Tour*, what did The Beatles travel in?
A32. A bus

Q33. In *Yellow Submarine*, what was John before he was John?
A33. Frankenstein

Q34. In 1995, The Beatles released a documentary. What's the name of the documentary?
A34. *The Beatles Anthology*

Q35. Which Beatle came up with the title to their film, *A Hard Day's Night*?
A35. Ringo. One night after a long, late performance, Ringo said, "It's been a hard day," and realizing it was night, added, "day's night."

Q36. What is the brand name guitar George played in the movie *A Hard Day's Night*?
A36. An electric 12-string Rickenbacker

Q37. In *Help!*, what color did Ringo have to be before he could be sacrificed?
A37. Red

Q38. Besides The Beatles, what other band performed in *Magical Mystery Tour*?
A38. The Bonzo Dog Band

Q39. In *Let It Be*, what did John say at the end of The Beatles rooftop performance?
A39. "I'd like to thank you on behalf of the group and ourselves and I hope we passed the audition."

Q40. In *A Hard Day's Night*, who is The Beatles manager?
A40. Norm

Q41. Who is *Help!* dedicated to?
A41. Mr. Elias Howe, the inventor of the sewing machine

Chapter 13
The Singles—The Songs—The Albums

An amazing feast for your ears, the desire to hear Beatles songs is endless! There's so many great songs and so many great albums!

"When it's only a Northern Song…"

Q1. What are the colors of the label on The Beatles singles released on Capitol Records?
A1. Yellow and orange, in a swirl pattern

Q2. Which Beatle sings "Do You Want To Know A Secret?"
A2. George. John wrote the song even though, as was the case with all John and Paul songs, it is credited as a Lennon/McCartney song. It was released as a single on Vee Jay Records, March, 1964 and reached number 2 on the Billboard Hot 100 singles chart. The B side was "Thank You Girl."

Q3. Who sings "Honey Don't"?
A3. Ringo

Q4. What song contains the lyric, "She's happy as can be you know, she said so."
A4. "I Feel Fine"

Q5. On which album is the song, "Devil In Her Heart"?
A5. *The Beatles Second Album*

Q6. Which Beatle sings lead vocal on "Devil In Her Heart"?
A6. George

Q7. What Lennon/McCartney song was given to Peter Asher and became a number one hit?
A7. "A World Without Love"

Q8. Name the song on the B side to the "Let It Be" single.
A8. "You Know My Name (Look Up The Number)"

Q9. Who is the walrus?
A9. This is a bit confusing. On "I Am The Walrus," John sings, "I am the walrus." However, on "Glass Onion" on *The Beatles* White Album, he sings, "The walrus was Paul." So according to John, there are two walruses—John and Paul.

Q10. What was the first Beatles song to use a sitar?
A10. "Norwegian Wood" played by George

Do You Really Know The Beatles?

Q11. "Ticket To Ride" is on the A side hit single. What song is on the B side?
A11. "Yes It Is"

Q12. Who plays lead guitar on "Get Back"?
A12. John

Q13. Who produced the *Let It Be* album?
A13. Phil Spector

Q14. Name the song that contains the lyric, "The wild and windy night, that the rain washed away."
A14. "The Long and Winding Road"

Q15. Name The Beatles record producer.
A15. George Martin

Q16. Who wrote the song "Till There Was You"?
A16. Meredith Wilson. "Till There Was You" is a song from Wilson's musical, *The Music Man*.

Q17. "Till There Was You" is on what album?
A17. *Meet The Beatles*

Q18. Who wrote "Twist and Shout"?
A18. Some people think The Beatles wrote "Twist and Shout." Some think The Isley Brothers wrote it. It was written by Phil Medley (perfect name for a songwriter!) and Bert Russell.

Q19. Who wrote "Honey Don't"?
A19. Carl Perkins. The Beatles loved, and still love Mr. Perkins.

Q20. "Honey Don't" is on what Beatles album?
A20. *Beatles '65*

Q21. Name the song that contains the lyric, "The way you treat her, what else can I do."
A21. "You're Gonna Lose That Girl"

Q22. What song is on the flipside of the single "Nowhere Man"?
A22. "What Goes On"

Q23. What record label released The Beatles single "Twist And Shout"?
A23. Tollie Records

Q24. On what date was The Beatles first US single released?
A24. February 25, 1963

Q25. Where did George write "Blue Jay Way"?
A25. In a house located on a street called Blue Jay Way in the Hollywood hills. The house belonged to Robert Fitzpatrick, who was The Beatles US attorney. George needed a private place to stay in Los Angeles, and Robert was out of town at the time.

Do You Really Know The Beatles?

Q26. On what instrument did George write "Blue Jay Way"?
A26. A small Hammond organ that was part of the furnishings in the house on Blue Jay Way

Q27. How did The Beatles come up with the album title, *Rubber Soul*?
A27. An American blues musician said that The Rolling Stones sounded like "plastic soul." The Beatles loved the phrase, and because their images on the cover were stretched and elongated, they came up with a variation of that phrase and called it *Rubber Soul*.

Q28. Where was the photo of the *Rubber Soul* album cover taken?
A28. On John's property in the garden at his residence in Weybridge

Q29. Which Beatle sings lead vocal on "Act Naturally"?
A29. Ringo

Q30. What was John's inspiration for writing "Being For The Benefit of Mr. Kite"?
A30. An old fashioned circus poster which he stumbled upon in an antique shop

Q31. What Lennon and McCartney song was recorded by The Rolling Stones?
A31. "I Wanna Be Your Man"

Q32. What is the name of the only Beatles song that uses a fuzz bass?
A32. "Think For Yourself," written by George. Paul added a fuzz bass track to his clean sounding bass line. Although somewhat obscure, "Think For Yourself," which is on the *Rubber Soul* album, is an outstanding sounding song, due in part to the fuzz bass.

Q33. Name the song that contains the lyric, "And the eyes in his head see the world spinning around."
A33. "The Fool on the Hill"

Q34. Who plays electric piano on "Get Back"?
A34. Billy Preston

Q35. Who is Billy Shears?
A35. Ringo, who sings lead on "With A Little Help From My Friends." The introduction sung by John, Paul, and George is, "Bil-ly Shears!" Billy Shears is also William (Shears) Campbell who supposedly replaced Paul according to the Paul is Dead hoax.

Q36. In "I Am The Walrus" what is dripping from a dead dogs eye?
A36. Yellow matter custard

Q37. Who plays the organ on "I'm Looking Through You"?
A37. Ringo

Do You Really Know The Beatles?

Q38. Who took the cover photo for the *Meet The Beatles* album?
A38. Robert Freeman. This famous black and white photo cover almost didn't happen. EMI, the UK parent company, which owned Capital Records, hated the cover. They thought it was too grim, too serious. Brian Epstein also didn't like it. He was afraid it would damage their image. Guess you could say they were wrong!

Q39. What was the name of the record label that released The Beatles first US single?
A39. Vee Jay Records

Q40. What inspired John to write "I Am The Walrus"?
A40. LSD

Q41. What song has "Strawberry Fields," "Lady Madonna," and "Fool on the Hill" in the lyrics?
A41. Glass Onion

Q42. What two English government officials are mentioned in "Taxman"?
A42. Mr. Wilson and Mr. Heath

Q43. What was the working title for "Hey Jude"?
A43. Hey Jules

Q44. Who sings lead vocal on "What Goes On"?

A44. Ringo

Q45. Name the songs on The Beatles first US single.
A45. "Please Please Me" and "Ask Me Why"

Q46. Why didn't the Beatles single on Vee Jay become a hit?
A46. Because Ewart Abner, the Vee Jay president, went to Las Vegas to celebrate his fortieth birthday, gambled and lost the majority of the company's operating and marketing expenses. Vee Jay had no money to promote the Beatles first US single release.

Q47. What is the name of the only Harrison/Lennon credited song?
A47. "Cry For A Shadow"

Q48. What two things are unusual about the album, *A Hard Day's Night*?
A48. It's the only US Beatles album to be released on the United Artists label, and it's the first Beatles album that has orchestral arrangements of their songs, orchestrated by George Martin.

Q49. What is the name of the only album by The Beatles that was recorded in the US?
A49. *The Beatles at The Hollywood Bowl*. It is a compilation of live performances that took place at

Do You Really Know The Beatles?

The Hollywood Bowl in August 1964 and August 1965.

Q50. Name The Beatles longest single.
A50. "Hey Jude"

Q51. What song on *The Beatles* White Album does Paul "sing" along with the bass track?
A51. "I Will." If you listen very carefully, you can hear him match the bass notes with his voice saying "do" or "to."

Q52. Name the song that contains the lyric, "But what you've got means such a lot to me."
A52. "Love You To"

Q53. Who plays the sax solo during the end section on "You Know My Name, Look Up The Number"?
A53. Brian Jones of The Rolling Stones

Q54. Who is the eggman?
A54. Even though John sings he is the eggman on "I Am The Walrus," the eggman is Eric Burden, who was the lead singer of The Animals. John heard about a ritual that Eric did while having sex with his girlfriends. He would crack open eggs on them.

Q55. When was *The Beatles at The Hollywood Bowl* released?

A55. May 1977. The delay occurred because the recording quality was poor. After a number of failed attempts to make the recordings commercially presentable, the task was given to George Martin who was able to clean up the recordings and produced the one and only official live Beatles album. (Even though there is the album *Beatles—Live at the BBC*, it was recorded in studio and not with a live audience.)

Q56. During the taped recording broadcast of "All You Need is Love," besides singing, what else was John doing?
A56. He was chewing gum!

Q57. What do the songs "Flying," "Dig It," and "Free As A Bird" have in common?
A57. All four Beatles are credited as writers.

Q58. Name the song that contains the lyric, "How can I ever misplace you?"
A58. "Long, Long, Long"

Q59. How many weeks was "Hey Jude" number one on the US record charts?
A59. Nine weeks

Q60. Name the only Beatles song written by John, Paul, and Ringo.
A60. "What Goes On"

Do You Really Know The Beatles?

Q61. How long is The Beatles longest single?
A61. Seven minutes, eleven seconds

Q62. What is the inspiration for the song "Lucy in the Sky with Diamonds"?
A62. John says it was inspired by a painting his son Julian did. Some believe it was inspired by LSD. Probably a combination of the two!

Q63. What songs were on the first Apple label single?
A63. "Hey Jude" and "Revolution"

Q64. What do the US *Rubber Soul* and *Sgt. Pepper's Lonely Hearts Club Band* albums have in common?
A64. No single was released. With no singles to play, some radio stations played the entire album! (The UK *Rubber Soul* contains the single "Nowhere Man.")

Q65. What instrument does John play on "Why Don't We Do It in the Road"?
A65. None. Paul and Ringo are the only two Beatles playing on that song.

Q66. What was the working title for "I Saw Her Standing There"?
A66. 17

Q67. Where did George write "Here Comes the Sun"?

A67. In Eric Clapton's garden

Q68. What is the inspiration for the song "Penny Lane"?
A68. A neighborhood in Liverpool

Q69. What was the working title for "Yesterday"?
A69. Scrambled Eggs

Q70. "Good Day Sunshine" was inspired by what Lovin' Spoonful song?
A70. "Daydream"

Q71. Who is the inspiration for the song "She Said She Said"?
A71. Peter Fonda, who whispered into John's ear "I know what it's like to be dead," while they were tripping on LSD.

Q72. Who bangs the anvil on "Maxwell's Silver Hammer"?
A72. Mal Evans

Q73. In "I Am The Walrus" who is climbing the Eifel Tower?
A73. Semolina Pilchard

Q74. Who plays organ on "I Want You (She's So Heavy)"?
A74. Billy Preston

Do You Really Know The Beatles?

Q75. Who is the inspiration for the song "Hey Jude"?
A75. Julian Lennon. Paul visited John's son who was sad—Hey Jules, don't make it bad…

Q76. Who plays the lead guitar solo in "Good Morning Good Morning"?
A76. Paul McCartney

Q77. What is the subtitle to "Norwegian Wood"?
A77. This Bird Has Flown

Q78. Who plays drums on "Back in the USSR" and "Dear Prudence"?
A78. Paul McCartney

Q79. What is the original title of the *Revolver* album?
A79. Abracadabra

Q80. What is the inspiration for the song "Martha My Dear"?
A80. Paul's sheepdog, Martha

Q81. Who is "Sexy Sadie"?
A81. The Maharishi Yogi

Q82. What songs did The Beatles record that are sung in German?
A82. "I Want To Hold Your Hand" ("Komm Gib Mir Deine Hand") and "She Loves You" ("Sie Liebt Dich")

Q83. Before Capitol Records released it, what label released "She Loves You" in the US?
A83. Swan

Q84. Paul plays the lead guitar solo on what song on *Revolver*?
A84. "Taxman"

Q85. Who recorded "Fool On The Hill" which became a hit single in 1968?
A85. Sergio Mendes

Q86. Who is the inspiration for the song "Dear Prudence"?
A86. Mia Farrow's sister, Prudence

Q87. Who was Paul trying to sing like when The Beatles recorded "Long Tall Sally"?
A87. Little Richard

Q88. What record label released the single "Cry For A Shadow"?
A88. MGM Records released it in 1964 after Beatlemania took hold in the US. It is the B side to the song "Why." Tony Sheridan, who wrote the song with Bill Crompton, sings lead vocal on "Why." The Beatles were his backup band, and they sing harmony. "Cry For A Shadow" is an instrumental with a few howls from John and Paul.

Do You Really Know The Beatles?

Q89. What are John and George singing in the background verse of "Paperback Writer"?
A89. "Frere Jacques"

Q90. Who plays piano on the "Revolution" single?
A90. Nicky Hopkins

Q91. What is the only Buddy Holly song recorded by The Beatles?
A91. "Words of Love"

Q92. What are Paul and George singing in the background during "Girl"?
A92. Tit, tit, tit, tit

Q93. George has four of his songs on which Beatles album?
A93. The White Album

Q94. What is the inspiration for the song "Strawberry Fields Forever"?
A94. An orphanage and property owned by the Salvation Army in Liverpool

Q95. "Mark 1" is the working title of what song?
A95. "Tomorrow Never Knows"

Q96. What does John say in the chorus at the end of "Baby You're A Rich Man" and who is it about?
A96. "Baby, you're a rich fag Jew." Brian Epstein

Q97. Which member of The Rolling Stones sang background vocals on "Yellow Submarine"?
A97. Brian Jones

Q98. What are the words in the chorus at the end of "I Am The Walrus"?
A98. "Oompah, oompah, stick it up your jumpa" and then mixed in with it, "everybody's got one, everybody's got one." Some people hear, "everybody smokes pot," while others hear "everybody's f**ked up." What do you hear?

Q99. What is The Beatles longest song?
A99. "I Want You (She's So Heavy)"

Q100. During the 1990's, what did The Beatles release that included demos, out takes, and previously unreleased recordings?
A100. The Beatles Anthology 1, 2, and 3

Chapter 14
The Paul McCartney Death Hoax

"He didn't notice that the lights had changed…"

Q1. When you play the beginning of "Revolution No. 9" backwards, what does it say?
A1. Turn me on dead man

Q2. When did Paul supposedly die?
A2. November 9, 1966

Q3. When you play the gibberish at the end of "I'm So Tired" backwards, what does it say?
A3. Paul's a dead man, miss him, miss him

Q4. How did Paul supposedly die?
A4. In a car crash

Q5. At the end of "Strawberry Fields Forever," in support of the death hoax, what does John say?
A5. I buried Paul

Q6. When you play the ending chorus to "I Am the Walrus" backwards, what does it say?

A6. Ha ha, Paul is dead

Q7. When Paul supposedly died, who replaced him?
A7. William "Shears" Campbell

Q8. How did The Beatles introduce Paul's replacement?
A8. On the segue between the opening "Sgt. Pepper's Lonely Hearts Club Band" song and "With A Little Help From My Friends" on the *Sgt. Pepper's Lonely Hearts Club* album when they sing, "Billy Shears."

Q9. When you play the chorus to "Let It Be" backwards, what does it say?
A9. He is dead

Q10. What track on the White Album has the sound of a car crash?
A10. "Revolution No. 9"

Q11. In support of the Paul is Dead death hoax, what does a voice say at the end of "I Am the Walrus"?
A11. O, untimely death, death!

Q12. What is a clue on the *Sgt. Pepper* album cover?
A12. It's a gathering in a cemetery at The Beatles grave site. The Beatles were dead and the new

band was Sgt. Pepper's Lonely Hearts Club Band, with William "Shears" Campbell (Billy Shears) replacing the deceased Paul McCartney.

Q13. What is another clue on the *Sgt. Pepper* album cover?
A13. The fresh grave is covered with flowers in the shape of a bass guitar.

Q14. According to the death hoax, why was the album called *Sgt. Pepper's Lonely Hearts Club Band*?
A14. Because John, George, and Ringo had lonely hearts and missed Paul.

Q15. What is another clue on the *Sgt. Pepper* album cover?
A15. Father McKenzie, who, in the song "Eleanor Rigby," wipes the dirt from his hands as he walks from the grave, is sticking out of the ground, looking at the floral bass guitar.

Q16. What is the clue on the inside photo of *Sgt. Pepper?*
A16. On Paul's jacket near his shoulder it has the initials OPD, which in England stands for—officially pronounced dead.

Q17. What is the Paul is Dead clue in "A Day in the Life"?
A17. The lyrics, "He blew his mind out in a car. He didn't notice that the lights had changed."

Q18. What is the Paul is Dead clue in "Don't Pass Me By"?
A18. The lyrics, "You were in a car crash and you lost your hair."

Q19. What is a Paul is Dead clue on the inside photo of the *Magical Mystery Tour* album of The Beatles dressed in white tuxedos?
A19. Paul is wearing a black carnation.

Q20. What do the opening lyrics to "She's Leaving Home" have to do with the death hoax?
A20. November 9th, 1966 was a Wednesday, the day Paul supposedly died.

Q21. What is another clue on one of the inside photos of the *Magical Mystery Tour* album?
A21. There is a sign in front of Paul sitting at a desk that says, "I Was YOU."

Q22. What clue does George give us on the back of the *Sgt. Pepper* album?
A22. He's pointing to the day and time of Paul's death.

Q23. What is a Paul is Dead clue on the *Abbey Road* album?
A23. The license plate on the VW Beetle says 28 IF. If Paul was alive then, he would have been 28.

Do You Really Know The Beatles?

Q24. What is another clue on the *Abbey Road* album?
A24. On the back cover, if you connect the circles on the wall before Beatles, it's in the shape of a 3. Three Beatles, not four.

Q25. What is a Paul is Dead clue on the *Let It Be* album?
A25. The background color of John, George and Ringo's photos are white. Paul's is blood red.

Q26. Where did a *Life Magazine* reporter find Paul alive?
A26. On his farm in Scotland

Chapter 15
Finish The Lyrics

"Words are floating out…"

1. I once had a girl, or should I say…she once had me
2. And she called herself Lil, but everyone knew her as…Nancy
3. Silently closing her bedroom door, leaving a note…that she hoped would say more
4. Going to work, don't want to go feeling…low down
5. I've got no time for you right now…don't bother me
6. Carve your number on my wall and maybe you will…get a call from me
7. Waits at the window, wearing the face that she keeps…in a jar by the door
8. I've got a chip on my shoulder that's…bigger than my feet
9. Your lips are moving…I cannot hear
10. And these memories lose their meaning when I…think of love as something new
11. Tried to please her, she only played…one-night stands
12. A crowd of people turned away, but I…just had to look

13. Your voice is soothing…but the words aren't clear

14. Pools of sorrow, waves of joy are…drifting through my opened mind

15. A, B, C, D, can I…bring my friend to tea?

16. Nothing you can say, but you can learn…how to play the game

17. Bright are the stars that shine…dark is the sky

18. You say you've seen seven wonders and your…bird is green

19. She's sweeter than all the girls and…I've met quite a few

20. If you're feeling sorry and sad, I really…sympathize

21. What did you see when you were there? Nothing…that doesn't show

22. I think of her, but she…thinks only of him

23. Leave it till tomorrow to unpack my case, honey…disconnect the phone

24. Buys every rock and roll book on the…magazine stand

25. Finally made the plane into Paris, honeymooning…down by the Seine

26. Ask a policeman on the street. There's…so many there to meet

27. The Hendersons will dance and sing as…Mr. Kite flies through the ring

28. Take these sunken eyes and…learn to see

29. Say you don't need no diamond rings and…I'll be satisfied

30. I never give you my pillow, I only send you…my invitations

31. One and one and one is three, got to be good looking…'cause he's so hard to see

32. The queen was in the playroom painting pictures for…the children's holiday

33. The clouds will be a daisy chain, so…let me see you smile again

34. And though the holes are rather small…they had to count them all

35. You didn't run, you didn't hide, you knew I wanted…just to hold you

36. Saving up your money for a rainy day, giving all your…clothes to charity

37. She'll never hurt me, she won't desert me…she's an angel sent to me

38. Don't pay money just to see yourself with…Dr. Robert

39. Lying with his eyes while his hands are busy…working over time

40. Working for peanuts is all very fine…but I can show you a better time

41. Love you everyday girl…always on my mind

42. I'm taking the time for a number of things that…weren't important yesterday

43. The man with a thousand voices…talking perfectly loud

44. She takes her time and doesn't feel she has to hurry…she no longer needs you

45. And she promises the earth to me and I believe her…after all this time I don't know why

46. All the girls around her say she's got it coming…but she gets it while she can

47. Me used to be angry young man…me hiding me head in the sand

48. Looking through the bent backed tulips to see…how the other half lives

49. She feels good, she knows she's looking fine…I'm so proud to know that she is mine

50. Well you may be a lover but…you ain't no dancer

51. If you're listening to this song, you may think…the chords are going wrong

52. The girl that's driving me mad…is going away

53. When I hold you in my arms and I feel…my finger on your trigger

54. You think you know me but…you haven't got a clue

55. You'll have to have them all pulled out after…the Savoy truffle

56. It's a thousand pages, give or take a few…I'll be writing more in a week or two

57. When I get near you…the games begin to drag me down

58. I would remember all the things we planned…understand it's true, yes it is it's true

59. Listen to me one more time…how can I get through?

60. Try to realize it's all within yourself…no one else can make you change

Chapter 16
The Solo Years

The stigma was so strong. Even though they had split up, once a Beatle, always a Beatle, whether they liked it or not!

Q1. What was John's first solo single?
A1. "Give Peace a Chance"

Q2. What color is the Apple label on the *All Things Must Pass* LP?
A2. Orange

Q3. What was Paul's first solo single?
A3. "Another Day"

Q4. In 1974, John Lennon made a guest appearance at Madison Square Garden. Who did he perform with?
A4. Elton John

Q5. How many records are in George's *All Things Must Pass* LP?
A5. Three

Q6. What's the name of Ringo's first solo single?
A6. "Beaucoups of Blue"

Q7. Where did Paul record his *RAM* LP?
A7. At A&R Recording Studios, NYC

Q8. What was John's second solo single?
A8. "Cold Turkey"

Q9. Who produced the *All Things Must Pass* LP?
A9. George Harrison and Phil Spector

Q10. What Ringo single can be interpreted as an attack on Paul?
A10. "Back Off Boogaloo"

Q11. Who plays lead guitar on "Cold Turkey"?
A11. Eric Clapton

Q12. Name the song on the flipside of Paul's "Another Day" single
A12. "Oh Woman, Oh Why"

Q13. Where was John's first concert performance without The Beatles?
A13. Toronto, Canada

Q14. There's one song written by George and Bob Dylan on the *All Things Must Pass* LP. Name the song.
A14. "I'd Have You Anytime"

Q15. What's the name of the band Paul formed in 1971?
A15. Wings

Do You Really Know The Beatles?

Q16. What is the name of the band John formed while The Beatles were still officially together?
A16. The Plastic Ono Band

Q17. What solo song did John release in February, 1970?
A17. "Instant Karma"

Q18. Who is the grand old painter Paul sings about on the *Band on the Run* LP?
A18. Picasso

Q19. What is the color of the Apple label on John's *Plastic Ono Band* LP?
A19. Grey

Q20. What was George's second US single release?
A20. "What is Life"

Q21. Why is there an explosive sound at the end of "Remember"?
A21. Before the explosion, John says, "The fifth of November," which in England is Guy Fawkes Day.

Q22. What is the name of George's second solo LP?
A22. *Electronic Sound*

Q23. Who plays drums on the "Instant Karma" single?
A23. Alan White

Q24. What three songs did John play at Madison Square Garden in 1974?
A24. "Whatever Gets You Through the Night," "Lucy in the Sky with Diamonds," and
"I Saw Her Standing There"

Q25. Who plays piano on "God" on the *Plastic Ono Band* LP?
A25. Billy Preston

Q26. What is the name of the club John got thrown out of in 1974 in West Los Angeles?
A26. The Troubadour

Q27. What's the name of the single from Paul's *RAM* LP?
A27. "Uncle Albert/Admiral Halsey"

Q28. What solo John song references Paul's death hoax?
A28. "How Do You Sleep"

Q29. What's the name of Ringo's second solo single?
A29. "It Don't Come Easy"

Do You Really Know The Beatles?

Q30. Who are the original band members of Wings?
A30. Paul, Linda McCartney, Denny Seiwell, and Denny Laine

Q31. Where was "Give Peace A Chance" recorded?
A31. In John and Yoko's bedroom at the Queen Elizabeth Hotel in Montreal, Canada

Q32. Who wrote "It Don't Come Easy"?
A32. Ringo and George

Q33. What hit single by Paul and Wings is on the *Red Rose Speedway* LP?
A33. "My Love"

Q34. What is the second single released from the *Double Fantasy* album?
A34. "Woman"

Q35. Which solo Beatle album is the closest to a Beatles reunion and has all four Beatles on it?
A35. Ringo's album, *RINGO*

Q36. Who produced "It Don't Come Easy?"
A36. George Harrison

Q37. What Lennon/McCartney song did Elton John record and release as a single?
A37. "Lucy in the Sky with Diamonds"

Q38. George was slapped with a lawsuit because of what solo song?
A38. "My Sweet Lord"

Q39. Who played piano on "It Don't Come Easy"?
A39. Stephen Stills

Q40. On George's *The Concert For Bangladesh* LP and at the concert, there were two drummers. Ringo was one, who was the other?
A40. Jim Keltner

Q41. What's another word for George's song "Wah-Wah"?
A41. Headache

Q42. Where did John celebrate his 31st birthday?
A42. Syracuse, New York

Q43. Who produced "Photograph"?
A43. Richard Perry

Q44. In addition to John, who else plays acoustic guitar on "Give Peace A Chance"?
A44. Tommy Smothers

Q45. Who wrote "Photograph"?
A45. Ringo and George

Q46. Where was *The Concert for Bangladesh* performed and recorded?
A46. Madison Square Garden, New York City

Q47. Paul recorded some of the *Tug of War* album on what island?
A47. The island of Montserrat

Q48. Who was the opening act at *The Concert for Bangladesh*?
A48. Ravi Shankar

Q49. Who was with John at The Troubadour in 1974?
A49. Harry Nilsson and May Pang

Q50. "Listen to What the Man Said" is on what Wings LP?
A50. *Venus and Mars*

Q51. Where did John and Yoko record their *Double Fantasy* LP?
A51. The Hit Factory, New York City

Q52. "Silly Love Songs" is on what Wings LP?
A52. *Wings at the Speed of Sound*

Q53. When and where was John's last live concert performance?
A53. April 18, 1975, Hilton Hotel Grand Ballroom, New York City

Q54. On what label was *Double Fantasy* released?
A54. Geffen Records

Q55. Who sings "Ebony and Ivory" with Paul on the *Tug of War* LP?
A55. Stevie Wonder

Q56. What song was the first hit single from John & Yoko's *Double Fantasy* LP?
A56. "(Just Like) Starting Over"

Q57. What's the name of the song Paul wrote for a James Bond movie?
A57. "Live and Let Die"

Q58. Who produced the *Tug of War* LP?
A58. George Martin

Q59. Who sang the "No No Song"?
A59. Ringo

Q60. Who co-wrote and sings the hit song "Say, Say, Say" with Paul?
A60. Michael Jackson

Q61. According to George, what are Apple Scruffs?
A61. Beatle fans

Q62. What song did Paul write as a tribute to John?
A62. "Here Today"

Do You Really Know The Beatles?

Q63. Who produced the "No No Song"?
A63. Richard Perry

Q64. Who played rhythm guitars and sang background vocals at *The Concert for Bangladesh*?
A64. Badfinger

Q65. What LP is "Say, Say, Say" on?
A65. *Pipes of Peace*

Q66. Why was John thrown out of The Troubadour?
A66. Because he was heckling and swearing at Tommy Smothers who was performing with his brother Dick on stage.

Q67. What is the song on the flipside of the single "My Love"?
A67. "The Mess"

Q68. What song did George write as a tribute to John?
A68. "All Those Years Ago"

Q69. Paul's song "No More Lonely Nights" is in what movie?
A69. *Give My Regards To Broad Street*

Q70. Who is Dr. Winston O'Boogie?
A70. John Lennon

Chapter 17
And In The End

The Beatles couldn't "get back."

Q1. What was the first thing that happened that set The Beatles free from being a group?
A1. Brian Epstein's death

Q2. Which album signaled the beginning of the end?
A2. The White Album

Q3. Who was the first to temporarily quit The Beatles?
A3. Ringo

Q4. Was Yoko solely responsible for the breakup of The Beatles?
A4. No

Q5. After the *Magical Mystery Tour* album, as song writers, what had changed between John and Paul?
A5. They rarely collaborated on writing songs together and wrote most of their songs separately.

Q6. Who broke up The Beatles?
A6. The Beatles

Q7. What was the name of The Beatles failing clothing boutique?
A7. The Fool

Q8. When did The Beatles officially breakup?
A8. April 10, 1970

Q9. Why did Ringo temporarily quit The Beatles?
A9. Because Paul was telling him how to play the drums.

Q10. Who was the second to temporarily quit the band?
A10. George

Q11. What were the signs of The Beatles breaking up on The White Album?
A11. They no longer recorded as a band. Some songs were recorded without the other 2 or 3 Beatles.

Q12. Who did Paul want to manage Apple and The Beatles?
A12. Lee Eastman

Q13. What was the last album recorded by The Beatles?
A13. *Abbey Road*

Q14. Why was *Let It Be* released after *Abbey Road*?

A14. Even though the songs were recorded before *Abbey Road*, The Beatles weren't satisfied with the *Let It Be* album until after the release of *Abbey Road*.

Q15. Why did George temporarily quit The Beatles?
A15. Because he didn't like Yoko being in the recording studio.

Q16. Who produced the final version of the *Let It Be* album?
A16. Phil Spector

Q17. Who did John, George, and Ringo want to manage Apple and The Beatles?
A17. Allen Klein

Q18. What was the original name of the *Let It Be* album?
A18. Get Back

Q19. How did Paul know Lee Eastman?
A19. He is Linda McCartney's father.

Q20. What band was Jeff Lynne and George Harrison in?
A20. The Traveling Wilburys

Q21. What were the last two songs The Beatles recorded and released?
A21. "Free As A Bird" and "Real Love"

Q22. What did Paul think of the way Phil Spector produced "The Long and Winding Road"?
A22. He hated it

Q23. Who produced "Free As a Bird" and "Real Love"?
A23. Jeff Lynne

Q24. When The Beatles recorded "Free As A Bird" and "Real Love," was John in the studio?
A24. No, it was recorded after he died.

Q25. Where did John and Yoko live in New York City?
A25. The Dakota, West 72nd St. and Central Park West

Q26. Besides Jeff Lynne and George, who else was in The Traveling Wilburys?
A26. Bob Dylan, Roy Orbison, and Tom Petty

Q27. When did George die?
A27. November 29, 2001

Q28. What was the name of the memorial concert for George?
A28. Concert For George

Q29. When did John die?
A29. December 8, 1980

Do You Really Know The Beatles?

Q30. How did George die?
A30. Lung cancer

Q31. How did John die?
A31. He died of a gunshot wound

Q32. Where was George when he died?
A32. Los Angeles

Q33. Who shot John?
A33. Mark David Chapman

Q34. Where was John when he got shot?
A34. In front of the Dakota

Q35. Where is Strawberry Fields in New York City?
A35. Central Park

Q36. When was the Concert For George?
A36. November 29, 2002

Q37. At the Concert For George, who sang "For You Blue," "Something," and "All Things Must Pass"?
A37. Paul McCartney

Q38. Where did the Concert For George take place?
A38. The Royal Albert Hall, London

Q39. At the Concert For George, what songs did Ringo sing?
A39. "Photograph," and "Honey Don't"

Q40. At the Concert For George, who sang "While My Guitar Gently Weeps"?
A40. Eric Clapton

Q41. At the Concert For George, who sang "My Sweet Lord"?
A41. Billy Preston

Q42. At the Concert For George, who sang "Taxman"?
A42. Tom Petty

Q43. How did The Beatles record "Free As a Bird" and "Real Love" without John?
A43. They used an old tape of John singing and playing the piano.

Q44. At the Concert For George, who sang "Wah-Wah"?
A44. Eric Clapton and Jeff Lynne

Q45. What was the last song at the Concert For George?
A45. "I'll See You In My Dreams"

Do You Really Know The Beatles?

Q46. At the Concert For George, who sang "I'll See You In My Dreams"?
A46. Joe Brown

Q47. In honor of George, on April 14, 2009, Paul, Olivia and Dhani Harrison were in Hollywood for what special occasion?
A47. George received a star on The Hollywood Walk of Fame.

Chapter 18
Yesterday And Today

The Beatles are yesterday, today, and tomorrow.

Q1. Who was George's first wife?
A1. Pattie Boyd

Q2. Who recorded the Lennon/McCartney song "Bad To Me"?
A2. Billy J. Kramer and The Dakotas

Q3. Who was Paul engaged to but never married?
A3. Jane Asher

Q4. What brand name guitar did Paul play during the "All You Need Is Love" broadcast?
A4. A Rickenbacker bass

Q5. Who was George's sitar teacher?
A5. Ravi Shankar

Q6. Who was John's first wife?
A6. Cynthia Powell

Q7. How did The Beatles come up with the name Billy Shears?
A7. It was their way of saying William Shakespeare.

Q8. Who recorded The Lennon/McCartney song "World Without Love"?
A8. Peter and Gordon

Q9. Who is Ringo's second wife?
A9. Barbara Bach

Q10. Who is Sean Lennon?
A10. John and Yoko's son

Q11. Which Beatle wore glasses?
A11. John

Q12. What was the address of The Beatles Apple Corps Ltd. company?
A12. 3 Savile Row, London, England

Q13. Name George's second wife.
A13. Olivia Arias

Q14. Who was the link between The Beatles and Billy J. Kramer and The Dakotas?
A14. Brian Epstein. He managed both groups.

Q15. Who introduced George to Indian music?
A15. David Crosby of The Byrds

Q16. Where did John and Yoko get married?
A16. Gibraltar, Spain

Do You Really Know The Beatles?

Q17. Who recorded the Lennon/McCartney song "From A Window"?
A17. Billy J. Kramer and The Dakotas

Q18. Who is Stu Sutcliffe?
A18. John's friend who played bass guitar with The Beatles

Q19. Where did Donovan and The Beatles go together?
A19. They went to India together to study transcendental meditation with the Maharishi Yogi.

Q20. In addition to "World Without Love," what other Lennon/McCartney song did Peter and Gordon record?
A20. "I Don't Want To See You Again"

Q21. Who was Ringo's first wife?
A21. Maureen Cox

Q22. Who introduced The Beatles to marijuana?
A22. Bob Dylan

Q23. Who wrote the song "Woman" for Peter and Gordon?
A23. Bernard Webb, a pseudonym for Paul McCartney

Q24. What is the name of John and Cynthia's son?
A24.10 Julian Lennon

Q25. Which Beatle is left handed?
A25. Paul

Q26. Who was the link between The Beatles and Peter and Gordon?
A26. Jane Asher, Peter's sister. Paul was engaged to Jane.

Q27. Name the second solo album released by a Beatle while The Beatles were still together.
A27. "Unfinished Music No. 1: Two Virgins" by John and Yoko, released November 29, 1968.

Q28. What song did George write with Eric Clapton that was recorded by Cream?
A28. "Badge"

Q29. What Las Vegas theatrical production is based on Beatle songs?
A29. *LOVE*

Q30. Who did The Beatles meet in Germany who became a member of John's Plastic Ono Band?
A30. Klaus Voormann

Q31. While still a Beatle, Paul composed soundtrack music to what movie?
A31. *The Family Way*

Q32. Which Beatle has blue eyes?
A32. Ringo

Do You Really Know The Beatles?

Q33. Before The Beatles became famous, what European city and country did they perform in?
A33. Hamburg, Germany

Q34. When Paul moved to London in 1964, where did he live?
A34. Jane Asher's house

Q35. Who was the first Beatle to release a solo album while The Beatles were still together?
A35. George

Q36. Who performs the Las Vegas theatrical production based on Beatle songs?
A36. Cirque du Soleil

Q37. In 2001, Paul performed at fund raising events for what charitable organization?
A37. Adopt-A-Minefield

Q38. What was Billy J. Kramer and The Dakotas' first big hit that was written by Lennon/ McCartney?
A38. "Do You Want To Know A Secret?"

Q39. Who was a working girl, north of England way?
A39. Honey Pie

Q40. How did the Cirque du Soleil production of *LOVE* happen?

A40. George Harrison presented the idea to Cirque du Soleil founder Guy Laliberte

Q41. Who died in the church and was buried along with her name?
A41. Eleanor Rigby

Q42. Which member of Cream married George's first wife?
A42. Eric Clapton

Q43. If you're down, who will pick you up?
A43. Dr. Robert

Q44. Who mixed the *LOVE* soundtrack and CD?
A44. Giles Martin

Q45. Who is Paul's second wife?
A45. Heather Mills

Q46. Who has sea shell eyes and a windy smile?
A46. Julia

Q47. Name the first solo album released by a Beatle while The Beatles were still together.
A47. *Wonderwall* soundtrack album, released November 1, 1968.

Q48. Who is Giles Martin?
A48. George Martin's son

Do You Really Know The Beatles?

Q49. Who played drums with John at The Rolling Stones Rock and Roll Circus?
A49. Mitch Mitchell

Q50. What is the song "Cold Turkey" about?
A50. Coming off a heroin addition

Q51. What does Desmond take to get to the jewelers store?
A51. A trolley

Q52. Who is Beatrice McCartney?
A52. The daughter of Paul and Heather Mills

Q53. Who played bass guitar with John at The Rolling Stones Rock and Roll Circus?
A53. Keith Richards

Q54. Who is the all American bullet-headed Saxon mother's son?
A54. Bungalow Bill

Q55. Who wrote and produced the song "Come And Get It"?
A55. Paul

Q56. Who doesn't have a point of view, and knows not where he's going to?
A56. Nowhere Man

Q57. Who played lead guitar with John at The Rolling Stones Rock and Roll Circus?
A57. Eric Clapton

Q58. Who is singing in the dead of night?
A58. Blackbird

Q59. When the rain comes, what do they do?
A59. They run and hide their head

Q60. What song did John sing at The Rolling Stones Rock and Roll Circus?
A60. "Yer Blues"

Q61. Are Paul and Heather still married?
A61. No, they are divorced.

Q62. Who is the professional female photographer that took pictures of The Beatles in Germany?
A62. Astrid Kirchherr

Q63. Jojo left his home in Tucson Arizona for what?
A63. Some California grass

Q64. What college did John and Stu Sutcliffe attend?
A64. The Liverpool College of Art

Do You Really Know The Beatles?

Q65. For which Beatle album cover did Klaus Voormann do the art work?
A65. *Revolver*

Q66. Who came in, grinning a grin?
A66. Rocky Raccoon

Q67. What happened to Stu Sutcliffe?
A67. He died of a cerebral hemorrhage

Q68. Who is filling in a ticket in her little white book?
A68. Lovely Rita Meter Maid

Q69. Who produced and arranged "Those Were The Days"?
A69. Paul

Q70. Who is so good looking but she looks like a man?
A70. Polythene Pam

Q71. Who was Stu Sutcliffe's girlfriend?
A71. Astrid Kirchherr

Q72. Who is majoring in medicine?
A72. Maxwell Edison

Q73. Who plays drums on "The Ballad of John and Yoko"?
A73. Paul

Q74. Who has cellophane flowers of yellow and green, towering over her head?
A74. Lucy in the Sky with Diamonds

Q75. What's the name of Ringo's band?
A75. Ringo Starr and his All Starr Band

Q76. Who listens to the music playing in her head?
A76. Lady Madonna

Q77. Where did John meet Cynthia Powell?
A77. The Liverpool College of Art

Q78. Who are clutching forks and knives to eat their bacon?
A78. Piggies

Q79. How many children does Ringo have?
A79. Three

Q80. Who was The Beatles first music publisher?
A80. Dick James

Q81. What was she protected by when she came in through the bathroom window?
A81. A silver spoon

Q82. What does Paul do during the song "I'm Only Sleeping"?
A82. He yawns

Do You Really Know The Beatles?

Q83. Ringo and Peter Sellers co-starred in what movie?
A83. *The Magic Christian*

Q84. What does John say at the beginning of "Let It Be" on the album version?
A84. "That was 'Can You Dig It?' by Georgie Wood, and now we'd like to do 'Hark, The Angels Come'."

Q85. Who sings "Those Were The Days"?
A85. Mary Hopkin

Q86. What Apple recording artist recorded "Come and Get It"?
A86. Badfinger

Q87. What street doesn't Maggie Mae walk down anymore?
A87. Lime Street

Q88. How many children does Paul have?
A88. Five

Q89. Who says something at the end of "Helter Skelter" and what does he say?
A89. Ringo says, "I've got blisters on my fingers!"

Q90. Rose and Valerie are doing what in the gallery?
A90. Screaming

Q91. Before moving to The Dakota, where did John and Yoko live?
A91. 105 Bank St. Greenwich Village, NYC

Q92. In 1977, what band released an album that was rumored to be The Beatles?
A92. KLAATU

Q93. When the rain comes, besides hiding their head, what else do they do?
A93. They slip into the shade and sip their lemonade

Q94. What is the name of George's only child?
A94. Dhani

Q95. Who wrote the lyrics to "Those Were The Days"?
A95. Gene Raskin. In 1968, he was a singer/pianist in a lounge at a London hotel. One night, after singing "Those Were The Days," someone from the audience approached him and handed him his phone number. He said he really liked the song and he wanted a singer to record it on his new record label. He asked Gene to ring him up the next day. The man who approached him was Paul McCartney.

Q96. What do the Indra Club, the Kaiserkeller, the Top Ten Club, and the Star Club have in common?

A96. The venues where The Beatles performed in Hamburg, Germany.

Q97. What song was going to be released as a new Beatles single on *Anthology 3*?
A97. "Now and Then"

Q98. Mary Hopkin had a hit single written by Paul (credited to Lennon/McCartney. Name the song.
A98. "Goodbye"

Q99. Where and when did John meet Yoko?
A99. At the Indica Gallery in London, November 9, 1966

Q100. What Beatle song has some verses in French?
A100. "Michelle"

Q101. What does Ringo play on the US single "Love Me Do"?
A101. Tambourine

Q102. What did Seltaeb have to do with The Beatles?
A102. Seltaeb, which is Beatles spelled backwards, was the merchandising company that was responsible for the making of Beatle products such as wigs, dolls, lunch boxes, etc.

Q103. In 2010, who were the musicians playing in Paul's band?

A103. Brian Ray, Rusty Anderson, Paul "Wix" Wickens, and Abe Laboriel

Conclusion
The Final Question

Q. How did The Beatles sustain their popularity?

The Final Answer

A. They had the ability to reinvent themselves and evolve with innovation, and write and record timeless songs that forever changed the face of popular music and the music industry.

Printed in Great Britain
by Amazon